Letter From the Co-Founder

ANISA CRESPO

Welcome to Million Dollar Mom Inc Magazine.

This magazine was created for the woman who knows there is more inside her, more purpose, more power, more impact, and more wealth waiting to be claimed. It was built for the woman who has walked through fire, carried invisible weight, and still chose to rise, even when no one was watching.

Million Dollar Mom Inc was not born from ease. It was born from experience. From loss, rebuilding, faith, resilience, and the unwavering belief that women deserve access to rooms, resources, and representation that reflect their true value. I know what it feels like to come from scarcity, to navigate grief, addiction, fear, and financial hardship, and still hear a quiet inner voice whisper, this is not the end of your story. This magazine is a response to that voice.

We created this platform to amplify women who are building something real. Not just businesses, but legacies. Women who are willing to be visible, even when it feels uncomfortable. Women who understand that visibility is not vanity, it is responsibility. When one woman is seen, another finds permission.

Inside these pages, you will find stories that are honest, powerful, and rooted in lived experience. You will find women who have dared to believe that motherhood and ambition are not opposites, but partners.

Million Dollar Mom Inc is more than a magazine. It is a movement rooted in visibility, influence, and impact. Every feature, every article, and every cover is intentional. We are building a platform where women are not only showcased, but supported.

My hope is that as you read these pages, you see a piece of yourself somewhere inside. Maybe in a story that feels familiar. Maybe in a dream you have been afraid to say out loud. Maybe in a version of you that is ready to step forward.

You belong here.

Thank you for being part of this community, whether you are a reader, a contributor, or a woman standing on the edge of her next chapter.

With faith, gratitude, and belief in what is possible,

Anisa Crespo
Co-Founder, Million Dollar Mom Inc

Letter From the Co-Founder

NATOSHA NAVARRO

Welcome to Million Dollar Mom Inc Magazine.

If you are holding this magazine, there is a reason. Growth rarely happens by accident. It happens when a woman decides she is ready to expand beyond what once felt comfortable.

As a mom, a wife, and a serial entrepreneur, I understand the pull of ambition alongside the responsibilities of family. I know what it means to build businesses while raising children, navigating uncertainty, and continually evolving as both a leader and a woman.

Throughout my career, I have worked across multiple industries and coached hundreds of women. One truth has remained consistent: women thrive when they are supported, seen, and strategically guided.

Million Dollar Mom Inc was created to be that support.

Inside these pages, you will meet women who are building businesses, expanding their influence, and creating opportunities not only for themselves but for others around them. Their journeys reflect the real experience of entrepreneurship, the pivots, the lessons, and the resilience required to keep moving forward.

Visibility matters. When women share their expertise and their stories, they create ripple effects that inspire the next woman to step forward.

As a co-founder, my commitment is to ensure that Million Dollar Mom Inc remains rooted in value, integrity, and impact. We are not here to chase trends. We are here to build something meaningful that supports women in becoming financially empowered, strategically sound, and confident in their ability to lead.

Thank you for being part of this community and for contributing to a future where women rise together.

With purpose and possibility,

Natosha Navarro
Co-Founder, Million Dollar Mom Inc

Letter From the Co-Founder

WENDY AIMEE PORTER

Welcome to Million Dollar Mom Inc Magazine.

This magazine represents more than success stories. It represents courage. The courage to be seen. The courage to speak your truth. The courage to step into rooms that once felt inaccessible.
Throughout my journey as an entrepreneur, mentor, and leader, I have witnessed firsthand what happens when women claim their voice and their visibility. When women stop shrinking to fit expectations and begin expanding into their purpose, everything begins to shift. Not only in their own lives, but in the lives of the people and communities they serve.

Million Dollar Mom Inc was created to hold space for that expansion.
This platform exists to honor women who are building meaningful businesses while navigating real lives. Women who are balancing vision with responsibility, ambition with heart, and leadership with authenticity. Women who understand that wealth is not only financial, but relational, emotional, and generational.
Inside this magazine, you will find stories that remind you that you are not alone on this journey. That doubt can exist alongside courage. That clarity often comes after action. And that your voice carries value, even while you are still growing into the woman you envision.

Visibility is powerful. When women are visible, they are remembered. When they are remembered, opportunities begin to open. This magazine was created not only to showcase women, but to elevate them through intentional exposure, strategic amplification, and global reach.

As a co-founder, my role is rooted in encouraging women to step fully into who they are becoming. To trust their intuition. To honor their experiences. To lead with both confidence and compassion. Million Dollar Mom Inc is a reflection of what happens when women support women without competition, comparison, or limitation.
My hope is that these pages leave you feeling inspired, affirmed, and ready to take the next bold step in your life and business. Whatever season you are in, know that your story matters and your presence here is meaningful.

Thank you for being part of this movement and for helping shape a future where women are visible, influential, and impactful.

With belief in your brilliance,

Wendy Aimee Porter
Co-Founder, Million Dollar Mom Inc

AS SEEN ON Roku tv fire tv

MILLION DOLLAR NETWORK

For Women. By Women. About Women.

Welcome to Million Dollar Network — the first all-women, women-run media network built to amplify female voices across premium streaming platforms including Roku TV, Apple TV, Amazon Fire, and beyond.

Million Dollar Network is a global stage where entrepreneurs, leaders, and visionaries transform their stories into shows, podcasts, docu-series, and spotlight features watched by millions worldwide.

Stream now on Roku, Apple TV, and Fire TV!

WATCH NOW

MILLION DOLLAR

Mom Inc Magazine

TABLE OF CONTENTS

Front Cover Feature: Why the Women Who Were Told They Were 'Too Much' Are the Ones Changing the World By Thyra Newby..08

Back Cover Feature: From Bankruptcy to Building Digital Income: How Mellisa Jenkins Is Empowering Women to Rewrite Their Financial Stories................19

Stop Trying to Stand Out. Start Leaving a Legacy By Criss Madrigal..26

MARCH 2026 EDITION
MILLION DOLLAR
Mom Inc Magazine

TABLE OF CONTENTS

Stand Out or Stay Invisible: How to Write the Book That Makes You the Go-To Expert in Your Field by Mattie Murrey........32

The Three Rules That Turned Hard Lessons Into Million-Dollar Success by Deb Purvin........37

The Moment You Remember Who You Are by Lisa Stamper........43

The Silent Weight: Understanding Women's Mental Health in Today's World By Daarina "Nina" Jefferson........47

COVER FEATURE

Why *the* Women Who Were Told 'They Were 'Too Much' *are the* Ones Changing *the* World with Thyra Newby

Why the Women Who Were Told They Were 'Too Much' are the Ones Changing the World

By Thyra Newby

There is a quiet moment many women experience but rarely talk about.

It usually happens late at night.

The house is finally still. The emails have stopped. The responsibilities pause for a moment. The roles we carry as mothers, partners, professionals, caretakers, and problem solvers soften just enough for something deeper to surface.

And in that silence, a question rises.

Sometimes gently.
Sometimes urgently.

Why do I feel responsible for everyone else's emotions? Why do I feel guilty when I say no? Why do I keep shrinking to keep the peace? Why do I work so hard to be enough and still feel like the problem?

For many women, this moment feels confusing. On the outside they appear capable and strong. They manage careers, relationships, families, and expectations. They are the ones people rely on. The ones who fix things, organize things, smooth things over.

Yet inside they feel exhausted. Not the kind of tired that sleep fixes. The kind that comes from carrying emotional weight that was never theirs to begin with.

If you have ever asked yourself those questions, I want you to hear something that might change the way you see your life. **You were never the problem.** You were the one who learned how to survive. And survival, especially when it begins in childhood, shapes the entire trajectory of a life.

THE INVISIBLE TRAINING OF CHILDHOOD

Children are remarkably adaptive. They are wired to survive whatever environment they are born into. When they grow up in homes where love feels conditional, where emotions are unpredictable, or where conflict feels unsafe, they do not question the environment. They adjust themselves.

If keeping the peace brings safety, they become agreeable. If achievement brings approval, they become high performers. If expressing needs causes tension, they stop having needs. If speaking honestly leads to rejection, they become silent. And when they notice dysfunction others refuse to see, they are often labeled the black sheep.

These patterns are not weaknesses. They are survival intelligence. Research from the Adverse Childhood Experiences Study conducted by the CDC and Kaiser Permanente revealed that early trauma is far more common than most people realize. Nearly two thirds of adults report experiencing at least one adverse childhood experience such as abuse, neglect, or household dysfunction. Children do not consciously decide to become caretakers, peacekeepers, or perfectionists. They simply adapt to the environment they are in.

A CHILDHOOD SHAPED BY SURVIVAL

I was born in Manhattan, New York. My early life was shaped by poverty, instability, and constant change.

Eventually our family moved to Puerto Rico. The island was beautiful in many ways. The ocean breeze carried salt through the air. The sound of coquí frogs filled the night. The warmth of the sun touched everything.

But beauty does not erase hardship.

Food was sometimes scarce. My siblings and I climbed mango and avocado trees because that is how we ate. Later we moved back to New York, to the Bronx. Winters were freezing and summers were suffocating. Poverty followed us wherever we went. There were also experiences during my childhood that no child should ever endure, including sexual abuse by people who should have protected me.

Even though I did not have the language for it at the time, **my life had already become about survival.**

HOW SURVIVAL SHAPES YOUNG ADULTHOOD

When you grow up learning to survive instead of feeling safe, it influences the choices you make as a young adult. Like many young women who grew up in instability, I entered a relationship that mirrored what my nervous system already understood.

At first it looked like attention. It looked like passion. It looked like someone who wanted me intensely. But intensity is not the same thing as love. Over time the relationship became controlling. Then it became violent.

There was one night that changed everything.

We were fighting again. His anger was escalating, and once again I found myself being hit. But something unexpected happened in that moment. Suddenly memories I had buried came rushing back. I saw the faces of the men who had sexually abused me as a child. And in that moment a question surfaced with startling clarity.

If I had left home at a young age to escape sexual abuse, **how had I ended up here?**

For a moment everything around me felt strangely quiet, even though the fight was still happening. It was as if my mind had stepped outside of the chaos and was looking at my life from a distance.

That question would not leave me.

If I had run away from one form of abuse, **how had I walked straight into another?**

Until that moment I had never fully connected the two. I had told myself that leaving home meant I had escaped what happened to me as a child. I believed that chapter of my life was behind me.

But standing there in that moment, something painful and undeniable became clear. The patterns had followed me. The fear. The tolerance for behavior that should never have been acceptable. The belief that love had to be intense, overwhelming, or even painful to be real.

It was like watching pieces of a puzzle suddenly fall into place in a way I had never seen before.

I realized that trauma does not always end when the situation ends. Sometimes it quietly shapes the choices we make afterward. It shapes the people we trust. It shapes what we believe we deserve.

As a child I had learned to survive by staying alert, by adapting, by tolerating things no child should have to tolerate. But no one had ever taught me how to recognize safety. No one had shown me what healthy love looked like.

In that moment a wave of emotions rushed through me all at once. Confusion. Anger. Grief. But underneath it all was something else. A sudden clarity that I could not ignore. For the first time in my life I saw the pattern clearly.

I had spent years running from my past, but I had never fully understood how deeply it had shaped the path I was walking. And once you see something like that, you cannot unsee it. That realization did not fix everything in that moment. But it planted a seed. A quiet but powerful awareness that my life did not have to continue repeating the same story.

Something came over me that night.

For the first time, instead of shrinking, I fought back. Nearby there was an iron. Without thinking, I grabbed it and swung it. The impact knocked him off balance and forced him to the ground.

Adrenaline surged through me. I jumped on top of him and grabbed the cord of the iron, wrapping it around his neck. But just as quickly as the anger had taken over, another voice rose inside me.

"Thyra, this is not who you are."

I stopped. My hands loosened. I let go of the cord. **That moment became a turning point.**

WHEN SURVIVAL BECOMES LIFE OR DEATH

Leaving the relationship did not mean the danger ended. For months he stalked me. Eventually there was a period when it seemed like he had disappeared. One night I was sitting in a car with a friend.

He found us.

He pulled beside the car and raised a gun. The sound of the shot shattered everything. The bullet missed me. But it did not miss my friend.

My friend died in front of me.

For a moment, everything around me felt unreal. The world did not stop, but it felt as if time had slowed down in a way I cannot fully describe. Sounds became distant. My mind struggled to understand what had just happened. I remember staring, almost frozen, trying to process the fact that a moment earlier we had simply been sitting in a car talking like any other night.

And now everything had changed.

Shock has a strange way of protecting the mind. At first it was almost like my emotions could not catch up with what my eyes were seeing. Then the weight of it began to sink in. Grief. Fear. Confusion. And something else that many survivors carry but rarely talk about.

Survivor's guilt.

Why him and not me? That question replayed in my mind again and again. The bullet had missed me. But it did not miss him.

There were nights when I would lie awake replaying the moment in my mind, wondering if something I had done differently could have changed what happened. Trauma has a way of trapping the mind in those loops, searching for answers that may never exist.

For a long time, safety felt like an illusion.

Loud sounds made my heart race. Being alone at night made me uneasy. My body stayed alert even when the danger was no longer present. I later learned that this is how trauma often lives in the nervous system. The body remembers what the mind is still trying to understand.

But something else slowly began to shift inside of me. Witnessing death so closely changes how you see life. The small things that once felt important began to feel insignificant. The opinions of others mattered less. The pressure to please people who did not respect me began to lose its hold. I had seen how quickly life could change. And that realization brought a painful but powerful clarity.

Life is fragile.

Time is not guaranteed. And the years we spend shrinking ourselves to make others comfortable are years we can never get back. That moment did not heal my trauma.

But it forced me to confront a truth I could no longer ignore. If I had survived something that could have easily taken my life, then I needed to start asking a different question.

Not "Why did this happen to me?" **But "What am I going to do with the life I still have?"**

That question would slowly begin to guide the choices I made moving forward. In the days and weeks that followed, the shock was overwhelming. But over time something else began to grow from that pain. A realization that surviving comes with a responsibility. Not a responsibility to carry guilt.

A responsibility to live.

TURNING PAIN INTO ADVOCACY

During my healing journey I realized I was not the only woman who had experienced violence. As I continued therapy and began learning more about trauma, I felt a strong pull to give back in some way. I did not fully know what that would look like at the time. I only knew that the pain I had lived through had to mean something more than just surviving it. That was when I began volunteering as a resident advocate at a domestic violence shelter and sexual assault center.

Walking into that environment was emotional. The building itself felt quiet, almost protective, like a place where women could finally exhale after living in fear. I remember the first woman I sat with. She looked exhausted. Not just physically tired, but emotionally drained in a way that many survivors understand. Her voice was soft, almost apologetic, as she shared pieces of her story.

She told me about the years she had spent trying to make the relationship work. About the ways she had blamed herself. About how she believed if she could just be calmer, kinder, more understanding, maybe things would change.

As she spoke, I recognized something familiar. I recognized the weight of self-blame. I recognized the confusion that comes from loving someone who hurts you. I recognized the quiet question so many survivors carry inside themselves: What did I do wrong?

Listening to her story, I realized how deeply many women internalize responsibility for abuse that was never theirs to carry. That moment changed the way I saw my own story. For years I had believed that the violence I experienced somehow reflected something about me. Something I had tolerated too long. Something I should have seen sooner.

But sitting across from that woman helped me see something I had not fully understood before. **Abuse is not about weakness.** It is about manipulation, power, and control.

Many of the women I met at the shelter were strong, intelligent, compassionate people who had simply found themselves in relationships where those qualities were exploited rather than valued.

Their stories taught me something profound. Survival does not make someone broken. It means they found a way to endure circumstances that should never have existed in the first place.

In those quiet conversations, I began to see my own experiences differently. What had once felt like shame slowly began to transform into something else. Understanding. Compassion. **And eventually, purpose.**

I realized that sometimes the most powerful thing we can offer another person is not advice or answers. Sometimes it is simply presence. Sitting with them. Listening. And reminding them of a truth many survivors struggle to believe at first. *What happened to them was never their fault.*

According to the National Coalition Against Domestic Violence, more than 10 million people experience domestic violence every year in the United States.

HEALING AND RECLAIMING MY LIFE

Healing is not dramatic. It is slow. It is quiet. Sometimes it is painful.

For a long time I believed healing meant that one day the memories would simply disappear. That I would wake up and the past would no longer affect how I felt, how I reacted, or how I saw myself.

But that is not how healing works.

Healing is less about forgetting and more about understanding. Therapy became an important part of that process for me. For the first time in my life I began learning about trauma, about how experiences in childhood shape the nervous system, and how survival patterns formed early in life can continue long into adulthood. So many of the things I had once blamed myself for suddenly made sense.

Why I felt responsible for other people's emotions. Why I struggled to trust safety. Why conflict made my body tense before my mind even understood why.

I began to understand that many of the behaviors I had carried for years were not flaws in my character. They were survival strategies. My mind and body had learned how to navigate environments that were unpredictable and unsafe. Those adaptations had once protected me. But the problem with survival strategies is that they often continue operating long after the danger has passed.

Learning this was both painful and liberating. Painful because it meant acknowledging how deeply the past had shaped my life. Liberating because it meant something even more important.

If those patterns were learned, they could also be unlearned.

Healing did not happen all at once. There were days when the past felt heavy. Days when memories resurfaced unexpectedly. Days when fear or sadness appeared without warning. But slowly, something began to shift. Instead of seeing myself as someone defined by trauma, I began seeing myself as someone who had survived it. That distinction changed everything.

As my confidence slowly grew, I began rebuilding parts of my life that trauma had once made feel impossible. Education became one of the ways I reclaimed my identity. Returning to school as an adult was both exciting and intimidating. There were moments when I questioned whether I was capable, whether I belonged in those classrooms, whether I could truly succeed after everything I had experienced. But every class I completed became another reminder that my story did not end with survival.

It continued with growth.

I eventually earned my bachelor's degree, and later I completed my MBA. Those accomplishments were not just academic milestones. They were deeply personal victories. Each step forward represented something larger than a degree. They represented reclaiming my voice.

For so many years my life had been shaped by silence. Silence around trauma. Silence around pain. Silence around experiences that felt too heavy to share. Education helped me find the confidence to speak again. It helped me see that my experiences did not disqualify me from building a meaningful life. In many ways they had prepared me for it.

The more I understood my own healing journey, the more I recognized that many other women were walking similar paths. Women who had survived childhood trauma. Women who had endured abusive relationships. Women who had spent years believing they were the problem. I began to see that the story I once carried quietly inside me had the power to help others feel less alone. And that realization would eventually shape the work I do today.

It is slow.
It is quiet.
Sometimes it is painful.

But slowly something began to change.

I began reclaiming my life.

FROM HEALING TO PURPOSE

Women began sharing their stories with me. They recognized themselves in my experiences. My story was not just about surviving. It was about helping other women understand that they were never the problem either.

THE WORK I DO TODAY

Today my work is rooted in helping women understand something many of us were never taught growing up. Patterns do not begin with us. But they can end with us.

For many years I believed the struggles I faced were somehow personal failures. I thought if I could just try harder, be more understanding, or keep the peace a little longer, life would eventually settle into something stable. What I eventually learned through therapy, reflection, and years of personal growth is that many of the patterns we struggle with as adults are not individual flaws. They are inherited survival patterns.

Generational trauma is rarely discussed openly in families, yet it quietly shapes how people communicate, how they handle conflict, how they express love, and how they respond to fear. Children raised in environments where emotional safety is inconsistent often become the caretakers, the peacekeepers, or the ones who carry the emotional weight for everyone else. Those roles may help a child survive. But they often follow women into adulthood where they continue to overextend themselves, tolerate unhealthy relationships, and silence their own needs.

Breaking generational trauma begins with awareness. It begins with asking the kinds of questions many families avoid. Why do I feel responsible for everyone else's emotions? Why does setting boundaries feel like betrayal? Why do I feel guilty for choosing my own peace? These questions are not signs of weakness. They are the beginning of transformation.

In my work today, I teach women how to recognize the patterns they inherited and understand that those patterns were once survival strategies, not personal defects.
When a woman begins to understand this, something powerful happens.
The shame begins to loosen its grip. She begins to see that the exhaustion she feels did not come from being “too sensitive” or “too much.” It came from carrying roles she was never meant to carry alone. Breaking generational trauma does not mean rejecting family. It means recognizing where unhealthy patterns began and choosing not to continue them. It means learning to set boundaries without guilt. It means learning to trust your own voice even when others are uncomfortable with your growth.

And most importantly, it means understanding that healing yourself changes more than just your own life. It changes the emotional legacy passed to the next generation.

I teach this work because I have lived it. I know what it feels like to carry silence. I know what it feels like to believe you are the problem. And I know what it feels like to discover that the truth is something entirely different. When a woman finally understands that she was never the problem, she stops shrinking to make others comfortable.

She begins to live with clarity, strength, and compassion for herself in a way she may have never experienced before. That is where real change begins. Not with perfection. But with awareness. And with the courage to choose a different path forward.
Today my work is about helping women recognize that the roles they carried for years were never their identity.

But survival was never meant to be a permanent home. The moment a woman realizes she was never the problem is the moment she stops asking for permission to exist as she truly is. And when she finally stands in the truth of who she is, she becomes something powerful.

Not just a survivor.

But a woman who turns survival into sovereignty and helps others do the same.

For many years I believed my story was about survival. Surviving childhood trauma. Surviving violence. Surviving moments that could have ended my life. But over time I realized something deeper. My story was never just about surviving what happened to me. It was about discovering the strength to refuse the roles I was given and choosing something different. Every woman who begins questioning the patterns she was taught is already taking the first step toward freedom. The women who were called too emotional, too sensitive, or too much were often the ones who saw the truth first. And when a woman finally understands that she was never the problem, she stops shrinking to fit other people's expectations and begins building a life that is fully her own. That is how cycles change. That is how healing spreads. One woman at a time choosing courage over silence and sovereignty over survival.

Connect With Thyra Newby

https://www.livelifeempoweredcoaching.com/

Social Media

Thyra Newby
https://www.facebook.com/ThyraNewby

@live.life.empowered
https://www.instagram.com/live.life.empowered

Live Life Empowered
https://www.youtube.com/@LiveLifeEmpowered

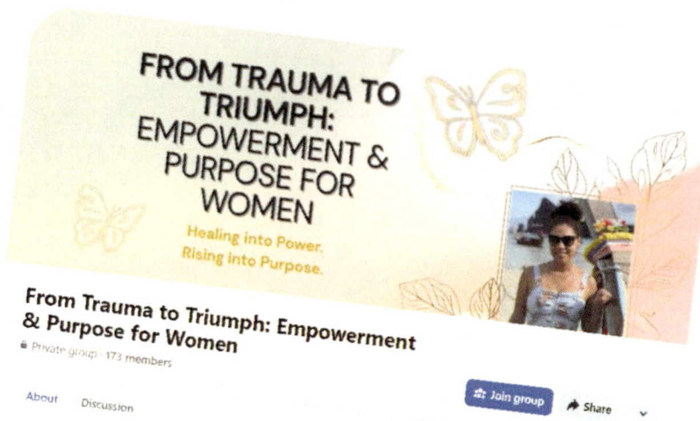

Join the free Facebook community:
From Trauma to Triumph:
Empowerment & Purpose for Women

JOIN THE GROUP

Photo credit: Larkin Newby | Revasonic Media

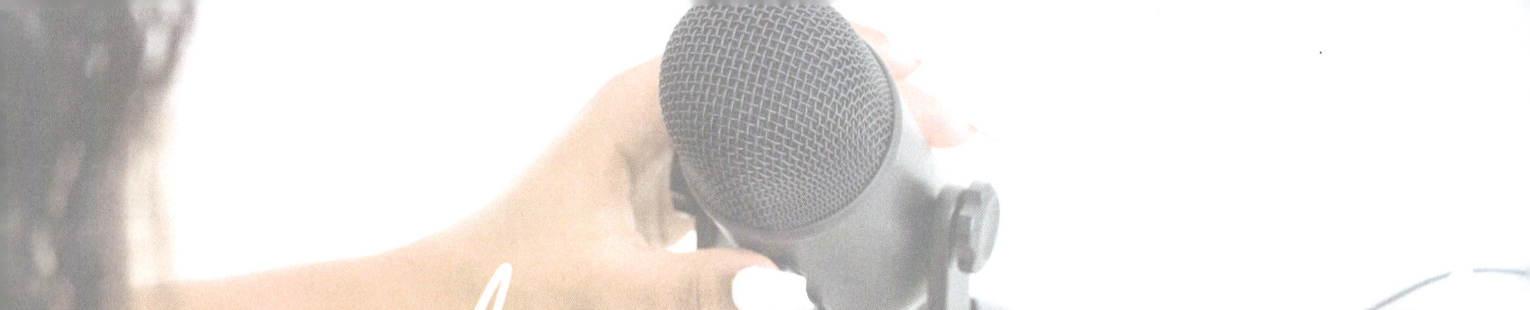

Media Mogul *Icon*

TURN YOUR **MESSAGE** INTO A TV **TV SHOW**

What if **your podcast**… **your expertise**… or **your voice** became a **television-style show** seen by **audiences around the world?**

Media Mogul is a **membership** created by Wendy Aimee Porter, Anisa Crespo, and Natosha Navarro ***designed to help women transform their message into professionally produced shows*** broadcast across the **Million Dollar Network**.

Inside Media Mogul, creators learn how to **expand beyond traditional content** and step into the world of streaming media… building a platform where **their voice can be seen, heard, and experienced on a larger stage.**

One example is Jay Kay, who is evolving her podcast *Many Wigs* into **The Many Wigs Talk Show**… **turning conversations into a visual show designed for global audiences.**

Because today, authority isn't just about having a message. It's about having a platform.

APPLY NOW

STEP INTO MEDIA MOGUL AND TURN YOUR VOICE INTO A SHOW.

From Bankruptcy to Building Digital Income:

How **Mellisa Jenkins** Is Empowering Women to Rewrite Their Financial Stories

For many women, the desire for something more often begins quietly. It starts with the realization that life isn't meant to be lived on autopilot—working tirelessly while dreaming about freedom, impact, and the ability to create a life on your own terms.

For Mellisa Jenkins, that desire eventually turned into a mission.

Today, Mellisa is a Women's Empowerment Coach and the Founder of Bossladies Girl Gang, a growing community dedicated to helping ambitious women build confidence, create digital income streams, and elevate their lives through entrepreneurship. But her journey to success wasn't always glamorous—it was filled with setbacks, lessons, and moments that tested her belief in herself.

Her story began in 2012 when she was introduced to entrepreneurship during her college years through a chance encounter with a Mary Kay consultant. At the time, Mellisa was simply a college student wearing makeup when a consultant approached her and asked what brand she was using. That brief conversation sparked curiosity and ultimately led Mellisa to begin her first entrepreneurial venture as a Mary Kay consultant.

In the beginning, business was exciting. Friends and family supported her, and she enjoyed selling products. But over time, she realized that the business model didn't align with the lifestyle she truly wanted. Managing inventory, hosting parties, driving around to deliver products, and constantly coordinating in-person meetings consumed more time and energy than she had expected.

Eventually, Mellisa stepped away and began exploring ways to make money online from home. However, without guidance, mentorship, or a clear roadmap, she found herself navigating the online business world alone.

Like many aspiring entrepreneurs, she turned to YouTube, Google, online courses, and countless training programs hoping to figure it out. Unfortunately, the lack of direction led to a painful reality—she was spending far more money trying to learn than she was actually making.

Over time, the financial strain became overwhelming.

After investing tens of thousands of dollars in programs and strategies that never quite clicked, Mellisa found herself frustrated, financially drained, and eventually forced to file for bankruptcy. It was one of the lowest moments of her life.

She had borrowed money from family members and even coworkers in hopes of making her entrepreneurial dreams work. When everything fell apart, the emotional weight was heavy.

"I remember feeling like a failure," Mellisa recalls. "I started questioning whether entrepreneurship was even meant for me. Maybe I was supposed to just work a job for the rest of my life."

For the next three years, Mellisa stepped away from entrepreneurship and focused solely on rebuilding her life. She worked diligently, repaired her credit, regained financial stability, and slowly regained her confidence.

But deep down, the desire to build something of her own never went away.

In 2019, while scrolling through Instagram, Mellisa came across a post that would change everything. The message invited women who wanted to "make an impact while making income." Something about it spoke directly to her heart.

The post led her to a mentorship opportunity with Wendy Porter through Crowned for Success.

Initially, fear held her back. When she first interviewed for the program in February 2019, she hesitated and walked away. At the time, her fear of failing again was stronger than her belief in herself.

But six months later, that same opportunity appeared in her feed again.

This time, Mellisa made a different decision.

"The money wasn't the issue," she says. "I had the same money in February that I had in August. The only thing that changed was my mindset."

She chose courage over fear and enrolled.

That decision proved to be life-changing.

Within just 60 days of completing the program, Mellisa had earned back her entire investment—and more. She began selling $2,000 coaching programs, connecting with women across the country and even internationally, and stepping into opportunities she had never imagined before.

She became a co-author of the international bestselling book Brave Women Stand, collaborated with 14 other powerhouse women, spoke on global virtual stages, and appeared on platforms reaching audiences across the Binge Network, Roku TV, Apple TV, iOS, and more.

More importantly, she discovered her true calling: empowering women.

In 2021, Mellisa founded Bossladies Girl Gang, a women's empowerment community focused on business growth, mindset mastery, marketing strategies, and helping women create income online. The community quickly grew into a network of hundreds of ambitious women who are committed to leveling up their lives.

Through her work, Mellisa began teaching women how to create digital products, grow their online presence, and build income streams that allow them to work from anywhere.

Then in 2025, another breakthrough moment arrived.

After noticing the rapid rise of AI-generated content across social media, Mellisa decided to learn more. She invested in AI training programs and began exploring how artificial intelligence could simplify and accelerate content creation.

Once she started applying the strategies, the results were immediate.

Her social media presence began growing rapidly, with new followers joining her platforms every week and profile views increasing by the thousands. Her AI-powered content began attracting attention from high-level entrepreneurs and seven-figure business owners, opening the door to collaborations, partnerships, and new opportunities.

Today, Mellisa teaches women not only how to build digital income through products and online platforms, but also how to leverage AI tools to create content faster, grow their audience, and position themselves as leaders in their industries.

Despite her success, Mellisa remains deeply grounded in her mission.

"I know what it feels like to struggle, to doubt yourself, and to feel like you're not meant for something bigger," she says. "That's why I'm so passionate about helping women realize they can create something different for themselves."

Her advice to women who feel stuck or uncertain about pursuing entrepreneurship is simple but powerful:

Don't allow past failures to define your future. Often, the difference between those who succeed and those who give up isn't talent—it's the willingness to keep going, learn, grow, and make better decisions along the way.

"Sometimes the only thing standing between where you are and where you want to be is a shift in mindset and the courage to try again."

Today, Mellisa continues to expand her impact by helping women around the world build confidence, grow their online presence, and create digital income streams that provide both financial freedom and personal fulfillment.

And while she's already accomplished incredible milestones, she believes this is only the beginning.

"I've come a long way," she says with gratitude. "But I truly feel like I'm just getting started."

Connect With Mellisa Jenkins

https://beacons.ai/bossladiesgirlgang

Social Media

@lissaliss_84
https://www.instagram.com/lissaliss_84

@bossladiesgirlgang
https://www.instagram.com/bossladiesgirlgang

BossLadies Girl Gang
https://www.facebook.com/bossladiesgirlgang

TAKE THE BOSSLADY PASSIVE INCOME POWER CHALLENGE

CLICK HERE

Meet the women behind the network

NATOSHA NAVARRO

Co-Founder, Visionary, Executive Producer

Natosha Navarro is a visionary entrepreneur, executive producer, and media architect with a bold mission: to build platforms where women are seen, heard, and remembered.

A former Air Force veteran turned six-figure digital marketing strategist, Natosha scaled her own business from the ground up before co-founding Million Dollar Media Group to create something bigger than a brand — a movement.

With a gift for positioning, proximity, and powerful rooms, Natosha leads the strategic direction of the network, curating high-level opportunities across television, podcasting, live events, and global streaming platforms.

WENDY AIMEE PORTER

Co-Founder, Media Strategist, Executive Producer

Wendy Aimee Porter is a respected media producer and founder known for spotlighting powerful women through high-level events and recognition platforms.

As a co-founder of Million Dollar Media Group, Wendy brings years of experience producing premium media experiences, red carpet events, and authority-building platforms for female leaders.

Her commitment to visibility, credibility, and curated excellence strengthens the network's reach and influence, helping create powerful stages where women are celebrated, recognized, and elevated.

ANISA CRESPO

Co-Founder, Brand Strategist, Executive Producer

Anisa Crespo is a powerhouse brand strategist and co-creator of Million Dollar Media Group. With a background in corporate leadership and high-level operations, Anisa brings precision, structure, and scale to the vision.

She specializes in helping women refine their positioning, elevate their messaging, and expand their impact through media.

Anisa is passionate about collaboration over competition and believes that when women build together, they build stronger. Inside the network, she plays a key role in brand development, show creation, and ensuring every opportunity aligns with excellence, strategy, and long-term growth.

Hit play on Roku, Apple TV, or Fire TV today!

WATCH NOW

Stop Trying to Stand Out. Start Leaving a Legacy.

By Criss Madrigal

There was a time when I believed influence meant standing out.

Being visible.
Being impressive.
Being recognized in every room I entered.

Like many ambitious women, I learned how to perform power well. I knew how to lead conversations and deliver value wherever I showed up.

From the outside, it looked like influence.

But inside, something felt misaligned.

I didn't feel like I belonged.

And when a woman doesn't feel like she belongs, she starts compensating. She works harder. She performs more. She tries to prove her worth in every space she enters.

Standing out becomes a strategy for survival.

But performance doesn't build legacy. It builds exhaustion.

My turning point didn't come from a bigger platform or a louder voice. It came the moment when the identity I had carefully built no longer felt like me.

I remember looking in the mirror and realizing I had become exceptional at performing influence, yet disconnected from my own voice.

That dismantling changed everything.

Instead of asking, How do I get more visible? I began asking a different question:

Where does my voice truly belong?

That single shift transformed the way I lead, the way I build community, and the way I show up in the world.

Because legacy is not built by standing out.

Legacy is built by belonging.

Belonging to your voice.
Belonging to your mission.
Belonging to the level of impact your life is meant to create.

We live in a time where visibility is easy. Anyone can post, share, broadcast, or build an audience. But being visible is not the same as being influential.

And influence is not the same as leaving a legacy.

Influence is frequency. It's the alignment between what you say, how you lead, and the energy you carry when you enter a room. It's the quiet certainty that comes when a woman stops negotiating her presence and begins embodying her voice.

You've felt this before. The woman who speaks once and shifts the entire atmosphere of a room. She doesn't need to compete for attention. Her presence creates gravity.

That's influence.

And when influence is rooted in truth, it becomes generational.

There's a bold, unapologetic energy I lean into. The part that refuses to dim her light in order to be accepted. It's the moment a woman stops editing herself and allows her voice to ignite something bigger than personal recognition.

It's about being anchored.

Anchored in purpose.
Anchored in identity.
Anchored in the knowing that your voice carries something meant to move through you and into the world.

When that happens, influence stops being about attention and starts becoming about impact.

And impact is what creates legacy.

This realization is what led me to create platforms that elevate women who are ready to lead from that place of alignment. Women who understand their voice is not random — it's responsibility.

Women who know they are no longer here to simply participate in conversations, but to shape them.

This March, I had the honor of speaking at Top 100 Women in Power, surrounded by incredible leaders who are each contributing their wisdom and voice to the collective.

And shortly after, I will be bringing together another powerful group of women inside Top 50 Voices of Influence — a space for visionary leaders who are ready to step forward, share their message, and influence conversations that shape the future.

Because they understand their voice carries something that matters.

If something moved within you as you read this, if you felt that quiet recognition that your voice may be meant for more, then perhaps this is your moment to stop waiting for permission.

Stop trying to stand out.

Start leaving a legacy.

And if you're ready to bring your voice to a stage designed for aligned leadership and generational impact, I invite you to explore what it means to be part of Top 50 Voices of Influence.

Because the world doesn't need more noise.

It needs voices that are ready to lead.

Connect With Criss Madrigal

https://www.crissmadrigal.com/

Social Media

@crissmadrigal
https://www.instagram.com/crissmadrigal

Soul Aligned Network
https://www.facebook.com/groups/soulalignednetwork

Photo Credit: Janessa Taber

Apply to Speak

ARE YOU A PODCAST CREATOR READY TO EXPAND YOUR LISTENER BASE AND REACH NEW AUDIENCES AROUND THE WORLD?

The Podcast Creator Channel on Million Dollar Network is a **curated media space** designed to **amplify powerful voices** through *professionally showcased podcasts* **streamed across major platforms including Roku TV, Apple TV, Amazon Fire, and more.**

MDN positions your show inside a **global network built for visibility, credibility, and growth.**

Your podcast becomes part of a **powerful lineup of women-led content** created to **educate, inspire, and influence audiences worldwide.**

Stand Out or Stay Invisible:

How to Write the Book That Makes You the Go-To Expert in Your Field *by Mattie Murrey*

You've spent years mastering your craft. You've got insights most people would pay good money to learn. But here's the uncomfortable truth: if nobody knows about your expertise, it might as well not exist.

This is what I call the Invisible Expert problem. Brilliant people with real knowledge, stuck competing on price, dependent on sporadic referrals, watching less qualified voices dominate the conversation and influence in their industry.

The fastest way to shift from invisible to undeniable? Write a book that positions you as THE authority in your space. Not just any book, but a strategically crafted one built on research and a proven formula.

THE EXPERT VS. VISIBILITY MATRIX

Think of expertise and visibility as two separate axes. Where you land determines everything.

High expertise plus high visibility = Thought Leader.
These are the Seth Godins and Brené Browns with deep knowledge combined with signature frameworks and contrarian positioning. They command premium pricing and have waiting lists.

High expertise plus low visibility = Invisible Expert. This is where most brilliant professionals get stuck. Amazing insights, but no platform, and playing it safe. The market undervalues them because the market doesn't know they exist.

Low expertise plus high visibility = Noise Maker. Surface-level content, loud promotion, trending topics. Short-term attention but no staying power.

Low expertise plus low visibility = Wannabe.
The goal is simple: move from Invisible Expert to Thought Leader. **A book is how you make that leap.**

THE RESEARCH THAT SETS YOUR BOOK APART

Here's where most aspiring authors go wrong. They start writing before they've done the homework that makes a book actually work.

Before you draft a single chapter, you need three things nailed down:
Your reader persona. Not "anyone interested in my topic." One specific person with specific struggles, specific desires, and specific circumstances. When you write to one person, you connect with thousands. When you write to everyone, you connect with no one.

Your competitive landscape. What books already exist in your space? What do readers love about them? What's missing? Where are the gaps? This research reveals the opportunity your book can own and the angle you can take ownership over.

Your unique selling proposition. What makes YOUR perspective different? What can you offer that no other author can? This becomes your north star throughout the writing process and your hook when it's time to market.

Skip this research and you end up with a generic book that blends into the crowd. Do it well and you've got a book that stands out before readers even open the first page.

THE FORMULA FOR A BOOK THAT POSITIONS YOU

Once your research is solid, the formula is straightforward:
E+F=B™ . Expertise + Framework = Breakthrough.

That's it.

Your expertise is what you know from experience that others don't. Your framework is the step-by-step method you can teach. Your reader's breakthrough is what they'll achieve by following your approach.

Every chapter should move your reader closer to that breakthrough. Every story should illustrate a point in your framework. Every piece of content should reinforce why YOU are the person to guide them.

This isn't about ego. It's about clarity. Readers want to know they're learning from someone who's actually walked the path.

WHAT CHANGES WHEN YOU GET THIS RIGHT

A book built on research and formula doesn't just sit on a shelf. It works for you.

It gets you invited to podcasts and stages. It gives prospective clients a way to experience your thinking before they ever reach out. It establishes your authority in ways that social media posts and networking events never will.

The difference between standing out and staying invisible often comes down to whether you've done the strategic work upfront or just started writing and hoped for the best.
Your expertise deserves visibility. Build the book that earns it.

Mattie Murrey Tegels is founder of My Own Ghostwriter, helping experts craft books that position them as go-to leaders in their fields. Learn more at myownghostwriter.com.

Connect With Mattie Murrey

1 hour book coaching: value of $200

BOOK IT NOW

www.myownghostwriter.com

Social Media

@myownghostwriter1
https://www.instagram.com/crissmadrigal

My Own Ghostwriter
https://www.linkedin.com/in/myownghostwriter/

My Own Ghostwriter
https://www.youtube.com/channel/UCeKk6RiLJnohjKJB5c57V8g

WOMEN OF *Influence.*

WHERE POWERFUL STORIES TAKE THE GLOBAL STAGE

Women of Influence is a premium television series featuring **visionary women** who are ***building empires, breaking ceilings,*** and ***leading movements across industries.***

Each episode reveals the *real story* behind success — the ***challenges***, the ***breakthroughs***, and the ***strategies*** that transformed ambition into impact.

Streaming globally across major platforms, the series gives extraordinary women the visibility their work deserves.

AS SEEN ON Roku tv fire tv

NOW CASTING
VISIONARY WOMEN
If you're ready to expand your influence and share your story with a global audience, this is your invitation to step into the spotlight.
APPLY NOW TO BE FEATURED
AS SEEN ON
Roku
tv
fire tv
WOMEN OF
Influence.
WITH YOUR HOSTS
NATOSHA, WENDY, & ANISA

The Three Rules That Turned Hard Lessons Into Million-Dollar Success

by Deb Purvin

THREE RULES I LIVE BY…

I've led an incredible life. I've been a successful executive, entrepreneur, adventurer and a mom. All demanding roles with responsibilities and rewards. I'm often asked, "What's my secret?"

Here are the three rules I live by…

First rule, be curious. People are incredibly interesting.

I traveled the world as a teenager skiing on the US Ski Team and then again as a parent of two small children (aged 1 and 6), my husband and I sailed through Central and South America for 5 years on our 42' sailboat. Both experiences led to incredible adventures. Obviously different cultures and beautiful settings, but what was most impactful were the people we met. Always asking questions. Even the commonplace ones, like where's the grocery store, led to longer fascinating dialogs.

People love to talk about themselves. Understanding what they do and why they do it has always intrigued me. What people tell strangers is even more amazing. These conversations always opened my eyes to ideas and patterns that later influenced my thinking – and my career.

In my 20 years as a banker, I asked questions every day of my borrowers. I love to hear their entrepreneurial stories! Now, as a business coach, I do the same thing.

Second rule, no regrets.

I grew two businesses to $100 million and sold them. But, as with everything entrepreneurial, there is always hard work and heartaches under the surface. My first venture was a real estate development company in which I built neighborhood shopping centers.

I was on my 8th development when all the banks in Texas went bankrupt in the late 1980s and they called all their loans. They made mistakes, but their borrowers paid the price. I defaulted on $82 million of debt. It took many, many years to repay it, but I was one of the few that did.

I even made a profit. It funded our sailing adventure.

But entrepreneurship was calling again and the bank that I had repaid was willing to lend me $100 million for my next venture I bought a ski and golf resort out of bankruptcy that had 2000 housing units permitted on 1000 acres. This was a very unusual permit because Vermont's land use laws are very restrictive.

I thought this would be the culmination of all that I had learned. In the first 18 months of ownership, I had almost $25 million in operating losses. It was awful! My first guest at the resort was the IRS. I owed $1 million in back payroll taxes with penalties and interest. The sewer and water plant permit required that I expand not only for my resort, but for the whole town (doubling my estimated $6 million cost).

I knew it would all work out because I was ready for the grand opening of the ski resort. Christmas week produces about 35% of my resort income. We had hired and trained more than 100 employees, were stocked with food and drink, and were ready to equip families with skis, boots, and snowboards. I'd spent $2 million making snow and the ski conditions were perfect. Every one of the 1000 beds in our beautiful Valley were reserved. The guests were arriving and excitement was in the air!

Until it rained. It rained hard – for two days! Everyone went home.

While I stood in the downpour, I had an epiphany. I realized I wasn't the only business owner in trouble. The whole valley was facing the same economic ruin. We needed to work together!

Our competitors, ski resorts owned by NYSE companies with big marketing budgets sold "ski packages." Their guests prepaid for their vacation – regardless of the weather. Could a bunch of independent business owners figure out how to do the same?

I gathered all the local owners to my empty base lodge. I proposed that we build our own "packages" by working together. I hypothesized that guests would rather stay at small family-owned bed-and-breakfasts with a cozy ambiance than stay at large institutional hotels. The same was true for all the amenities – snowmobiling, sleigh rides, sledding, skiing, restaurants, boutiques.

BUT, to make this work, we all had to agree on the economics. Could we choose price points guaranteeing each owner solid margins? Could we agree on a booking system that would be fair? Should we share client lists to improve the probabilities of success? Many topics had to be discussed and agreed upon -- a huge experiment with our businesses at risk.

Despite fierce discussions, 42 of us agreed to be part of the "Marketing Collaborative." Then, over the next several days, every single business owner in the "Collaborative" walked into my office and confessed that they had no idea what any of the financial terms meant! They wanted to move forward, but could I explain the concepts? How would they survive?

Now, not only did I own the largest asset in the valley, but I had to oversee the "Collaborative" and teach these business owners to run their businesses profitably. What a great idea I had!

We started meeting weekly -- partly to discuss marketing strategies and partly to learn business basics. Each week, members brought their financial and management questions to the meeting, I would pick one topic from their questions and develop a worksheet for them to complete for the next week's discussion.

In each meeting, we'd first discuss marketing issues (really, successes, for it was going very well), then we'd talk about our homework. We learned about each other's businesses, how to support and help each other, and how to manage our businesses better.

The Marketing Collaborative was an incredible success! My revenue doubled the first year and doubled again the following year. Everyone reported similar results. Our meetings became more about opportunities than challenges; more about helping each other as we became more profitable and confident in our own endeavors.

Within 6 years, each business owner had sold their company for more than $1M net! Me too…
I didn't know it at the time, but Business Owner's MBA (BOMBA) was born.

Third rule, own your leadership.

I had always been successful as an individual – skier, student, banker, developer. When I had to manage 150 employees, run a ski area and a golf course, build and sell townhouses, condos and homes -- and help 41 other business owners be successful, my mindset changed.

Listening for the unspoken challenges, gently guiding business owners to profitable solutions (even when they didn't like the ideas), learning about the issues that faced each different industry transformed me.

I was no longer just a successful individual, but a leader. Not a leader because I had the biggest asset, but a leader because I led with a passion to want us all to succeed! I started running my company with a different construct – from the perspective of others.

I wished I had understood this leadership mindset earlier in my career, but no regrets! It's how I help others be successful now.

30 minute financial audit

Connect With Deb Purvin

www.businessownersmba.com

Social Media

Deb Purvin
www.linkedin.com/in/debpurvin

THIS NOVEMBER...

The room that *changed everything* is returning

The MILLION DOLLAR Room

A *three-day experience for women* stepping into ***visibility*, *proximity*, *power*,** and ***expansion.***

NO DISTRACTIONS...

Just the room. The women. The work. The breakthroughs. The visibility.
Your next level... fully activated.

VIP General Admission

- Three full days of transformational sessions
- Keynotes, trainings, activations
- Networking and community
- Access to the Million Dollar Marketplace
- Surprise visibility moments
- First access to apply for speaking opportunities
- Be part of a media production filmed for a movie

Elite VIP Experience

- Three days in the front row
- Welcome Soirée
- VIP only experiences and activations
- VIP Lounge
- Priority access and concierge support
- Exclusive gifts and surprises
- Private VIP only session with special guests

Bigger. Bolder. *More unforgettable than ever.*

GET YOUR TICKETS
FOR NOVEMBER 2026

WITH YOUR HOSTS

NATOSHA, WENDY, & ANISA

The Moment You Remember Who You Are

by Lisa Stamper

Human beings are not broken. We've simply forgotten who we are.

For years, we've been taught that success requires constant improvement. More discipline. More productivity. More strategies to fix what isn't working in our lives.

If our careers stall, our relationships struggle, or our health declines, the message is often the same: work harder on yourself. Become better. Do more.

But what if the real issue isn't that we're broken?

What if we've simply been conditioned to forget who we truly are?

This realization changed the entire trajectory of my life.

Years ago, I found myself rebuilding from circumstances I never imagined I would face. I was living in a women's shelter, trying to create stability for myself while questioning how everything had unraveled.

In that season of my life, I believed what many people believe when things fall apart: that I had somehow failed.

But during that time, something unexpected happened.

I began listening to the quiet inner voice I had ignored for years.

The voice that said:
"This is not all there is to life. You are meant for more than just survival."

Following that voice led me on a journey that transformed everything. Over time, I rebuilt my life, created a thriving seven-figure business, and stepped onto stages around the world. My book, The Success Codes, debuted on the Nasdaq New York Times Square billboard and connected with readers globally.

But the greatest transformation wasn't external success.

Through my work today, I meet powerful women every day—entrepreneurs, leaders, mothers, visionaries—who have built impressive lives on the outside but still feel a quiet sense that something is missing.

They've done the courses. The strategies. The personal development.

And yet they still feel like they're carrying the weight of doing everything themselves.

What I've discovered is that most people are not struggling because they lack ability or intelligence.

They are struggling because they've been conditioned to disconnect from their own truth.

From childhood expectations to societal pressures, many of us learn to silence our intuition, suppress our authentic voice, and measure our worth by performance rather than alignment.

Over time, that disconnection creates exhaustion, self-doubt, and the feeling that we must constantly prove ourselves.

But the moment someone reconnects with their true identity, everything begins to change.

I call this process:

Remember. Reclaim. Rise.

First, we remember who we are beneath the layers of conditioning and survival patterns.

Then we reclaim our sovereignty—our ability to trust our intuition, set boundaries, and make decisions aligned with our truth.

Finally, we rise into a life that reflects that identity, where success, wealth, health, and relationships grow from alignment rather than pressure.

I have seen women go from burnout and uncertainty to building thriving businesses, launching bestselling books, healing long-standing health challenges, and creating lives filled with freedom, joy and purpose.

Not because they forced themselves to become someone new.

But because they finally came home to themselves.

The world doesn't need more people striving to fit into expectations that were never meant for them.

It needs people who remember who they are.

Because when a woman reconnects with her truth, she doesn't just transform her own life.

She changes the future for her family, her community, and the generations that follow.

And that's where real success begins.

Connect With Lisa Stamper

https://www.lisastamper.com + https://thesovereigncodes.com

Social Media

@lisastamperintuitive
instagram.com/lisastamperintuitive/

@intuitivelisastamper
https://www.tiktok.com/@intuitivelisastamper

Lisa Stamper
https://www.facebook.com/lisastamperintuitive

Offers

WHOLE
https://www.lisastamper.com/whole

ROOT TO RESTORATION
https://www.lisastamper.com/root-to-restoration

WANT TO **GET PUBLISHED** IN MILLION DOLLAR MOM INC MAGAZINE?

Million Dollar Mom Inc. Magazine is not just a publication. It is a **premium visibility platform created for ambitious women** who understand that influence is built intentionally.

Distributed digitally and in print through Amazon and IngramSpark, Million Dollar Mom Inc. Magazine **offers global accessibility** while maintaining a **luxury**, **high-level brand standard**. Contributors also benefit from **expanded visibility through our email marketing, social platforms, community ecosystem,** and **media network.**

Visit the website to learn more & apply to be published.

CLICK HERE

YOUR PUBLISHING OPTIONS:

PUBLISH AN ARTICLE	STRATEGIC AD PLACEMENT	BACK COVER FEATURE	FRONT COVER FEATURE
Thought leadership article, up to 600 word count	Place your brand inside a magazine aligned with leadership, influence, and impact.	Includes a high-impact four-page spread designed to showcase your brand with intention and authority.	The most premium placement, including a six-page spread and front-of-magazine visibility that sets the tone for the entire issue.
FREE	$97	$497	$997

The Silent Weight: Understanding Women's Mental Health in Today's World

By Daarina "Nina" Jefferson

Women carry worlds on their shoulders.

We are daughters, mothers, leaders, caregivers, entrepreneurs, partners, and visionaries. Yet behind the strength, productivity, and resilience, many women are silently battling anxiety, depression, trauma, burnout, and emotional exhaustion.

Women's mental health deserves more than awareness. It deserves attention, compassion, and action.

WHY WOMEN'S MENTAL HEALTH MATTERS

According to the World Health Organization, women are more likely than men to experience depression and anxiety disorders. Hormonal changes, societal expectations, caregiving responsibilities, trauma exposure, and workplace inequities all play a role.

But statistics don't tell the whole story.

Many women are high-functioning while hurting. They show up. They smile. They perform. Yet internally, they are overwhelmed, overstimulated, and emotionally drained.

THE HIDDEN PRESSURES WOMEN FACE

1. The Pressure to "Hold It All Together"
Women are often expected to be the emotional anchors of families, workplaces, and communities. When everyone leans on you, who do you lean on?

2. Hormonal and Biological Factors
Hormonal shifts during menstruation, pregnancy, postpartum, and menopause can significantly impact mood and mental stability. These are not "mood swings" — they are physiological realities.

3. Trauma and Unspoken Pain
Women experience high rates of domestic violence, sexual assault, and emotional abuse. Many carry trauma silently due to shame, fear, or cultural stigma.

BREAKING THE SILENCE

Healing begins when silence ends.

Women need safe spaces to speak openly about:
- Anxiety without being labeled "dramatic"
- Depression without being called "ungrateful"
- Exhaustion without being called "lazy"
- Boundaries without being called "selfish"

Mental health is not a weakness. It is health.

PRACTICAL STEPS TOWARD HEALING

- Normalize therapy. Seeking help is strength, not failure.
- Build a support circle. Even one safe person makes a difference.
- Prioritize rest. Rest is not a reward — it is a necessity.
- Set boundaries. You cannot pour from an empty cup.
- Tell your story. Your voice may be someone else's survival guide.

A GLOBAL CALL TO CARE

Women's mental health is not just a personal issue — it is a public health issue. When women are mentally well, families thrive, businesses grow, and communities strengthen.

We must move from silence to support.
From stigma to understanding.
From surviving to healing.

Because strong women deserve strong support systems.

And no woman should suffer in silence.

Connect With Daarina Jefferson

Social Media

@daarinajefferson
www.instagram.com/daarinajefferson

Daarina Jefferson
https://www.linkedin.com/in/daarina-jefferson-8301b6199/

Daarina Jefferson
www.facebook.com/daarina.jefferson

www.ingramcontent.com/pod-product-compliance
Lightning Source LLC
LaVergne TN
LVRC080248220926
848482LV00042B/351

* 9 7 9 8 9 9 5 2 1 6 6 1 2 *